Guide to
BIDDING

Devising and structuring projects for grant funding

Jenny Middleton

Middlesex
University
PRESS

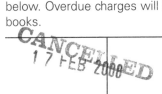

Guide to Bidding

This is a book about funding – identifying and winning funding for your project and your organisation. It will be relevant to any organisation that is working, or plans to work, for the benefit of the people or businesses in their area. In short, it is a guide to help those who want to access regeneration funding of one kind or another – Lottery, European Social Fund, local grants and funds and so on.

The book does not cover commercial tendering, although many of the techniques and tips are relevant and would be helpful in putting a tender together. Furthermore, it is aimed more at bidding for project funding rather than bidding for core funding for an organisation.

The purpose of this book is to be a practical guide. As you read through the book you will find questions and exercises in italics. Working through these in order will help you to develop a good project plan and to write your bid. You can either work through these alone or as part of a team. For a partnership project you may want to use the exercises as part of a structured partnership development.

First published in 2004 by Middlesex University Press

ISBN 1 898253 89 7

A CIP catalogue record for this book is available from
The British Library

Design by Helen Taylor

Printed and bound in Malta by Gutenberg Press Limited

Middlesex University Press, Queensway, Enfield, Middlesex EN3 4SA

Tel: +44 (0)20 8411 5734 Fax: +44 (0)20 8411 5736

www.mupress.co.uk

Contents

CHAPTER ONE

Funding
for beginners

Don't panic!

If you are completely new to funding, the first thing to remember is not to panic! Like any business, the business of finding, winning and working with regeneration funding has its own practices, customs and jargon but finding your way through need not be a nightmare. This chapter is designed to give you the basics – guidance on finding funding, an introduction to some of the major funds and the terms used to talk about them.

The jargon

It is difficult to create a comprehensive jargon-buster for funding, simply because there is such a wide variety of funding sources and they are all different. However, some of the common terms that are used are listed below.

The bid is the document that you submit to the funding body. Usually it will consist of a completed form, and sometimes will have other documents attached such as your organisation's accounts. It is not to be confused with **the project** which is the activity that you will be carrying out if you are successful. The bid describes the project and makes the case for it to be funded.

A **funding body** is an organisation that distributes funds to individual projects. Funding bodies include government departments, Government Offices for the Regions, individual charitable trusts, Regional Development Agencies, other National bodies such as the National Lottery, Learning and Skills Councils and JobCentre Plus, to name but a few!

The bidding process is often organised into **funding rounds** (also known as **bidding rounds**) – specific times at which you can submit bids to apply for the funding. Deadline dates and times can be very strict.

Bids are often assessed by some kind of **scoring panel** – a group of people who have been brought together to assess the bids against a **scoring framework**. They will work individually or together to arrive at a score for each section or answer on the form, and add up the score for each bid. This score is then used to decide which bids are funded – in general the highest scoring bids are funded, working down the list until all available funding has been used up. Where this system is used, the funding body will usually publish the scoring framework in advance so that those writing the bid can ensure that they cover the right things in their answer. The scoring framework will include a number of **criteria** for each question or section of the form, and this is sometimes quite detailed. Not all bids are assessed this way. Organisations that give away relatively small sums of money (e.g. charitable trusts) may consider all the funding applications at a board meeting or similar, and will not use a scoring framework.

A **beneficiary** is someone who benefits from the project in some way. A beneficiary can be an individual person or a whole organisation. Some grant funding schemes may use other words in place of beneficiary, such as 'client'. As a general rule, when writing a bid you should try to use the same jargon as the funders use in their guidelines and other documents.

Most funds require you to **target** a particular group of people as beneficiaries. In fact some funds will only support projects that work with a certain groups, for example refugees, or young people.

Outputs can also be referred to as outcomes. Basically, an output or outcome is a project's achievement or end result. Some funders will be looking for particular types of outputs (for example, people achieving qualifications), whereas others are more flexible. Outputs may be either **hard** or **soft**. A hard output is something you can easily measure and can tell when it has been achieved, for example the number of people moving into employment or the number of businesses starting up. A soft output is more difficult to measure, although there are ways to measure them. It usually relates to the achievements of an individual beneficiary, for example increased confidence. Many charitable trusts will expect soft outputs, though they may not call them this.

Some funds will not cover 100% of project costs, but only a smaller percentage. For example the European Social Fund will usually only cover up to 45% of project costs. The rest of the money has to be found from other sources and is known as **match funding**. Match funding can come from another grant funding source (although there may be restrictions on this), from your own organisational funds or from partner organisations. Some of the match funding may be **in kind** – the donation of resources such as staff and equipment rather than actual cash.

SMEs are small and medium sized enterprises, companies employing fewer than 250 people. A lot of funding is targeted at helping SMEs, so it is a term you are likely to come across in funding documents.

Finding funding for your project

Unless you already have a fund in mind that you want to apply to, finding a source of funding for your project will require some research. One way to find a suitable funding body is to ask around – look at other similar projects and organisations and find out how they are funded.

Another is to ask for advice from an agency in your local area or region:

- For projects involving training and learning activities, the Learning and Skills Council (LSC) for your area, or Learning Partnership. See **www.lsc.gov.uk** or phone 0870 900 6800 for information on your local LSC. Your Local Authority or LSC should be able to put you in touch with the Learning Partnership for your area.

- For projects aimed at businesses, or involving capital investment (e.g. new buildings), the Government Office for the region or Regional Development Agency (England); Welsh Development Agency (Wales); Scottish Executive or one of the Scottish European Partnerships (Scotland).

- For projects with a charitable or social aim, your local or regional council for voluntary services. A list of these can be found at **www.nacvs.org.uk/cvsdir/**

You could also use the internet to find funding sources. Good places to start are:

Government Funding website:

www.governmentfunding.org.uk
This is a very comprehensive guide to finding funding for voluntary and community sector organisations from government departments

Access Funds:

www.access-funds.co.uk
This is a directory of grants, mainly aimed at the voluntary sector. Although the main body of the site covers England only, they do have directories for Scotland and Wales.

European Social Fund Unit:

www.esf.gov.uk
Information about the European Social Fund in Great Britain.

See also information about the European Regional Development Fund:

www.urban.odpm.gov.uk/programmes/erdf/

Information on European Funding in Scotland, Wales and Northern Ireland can be found at:

www.scotland.gov.uk/esf

www.dedni.gov.uk/european_programmes/

www.wefo.wales.gov.uk/

National Lottery Good Causes:

www.lotterygoodcauses.org.uk

Information about all the different strands of National Lottery grant funding.

Assessing funds for suitability

Not all funds are suitable for all projects, and you will need to look at your project and your organisation to assess which funds would be worth submitting a bid to. Points to consider when looking for a source of funding are:

- **The status of your organisation** Some funds require that you are a registered charity, others that you are a public sector body. There are many kinds of funding that are open to organisations from all sectors, but most require that you are legally constituted in some way and you may need to show proof of this.

- **How much funding do you need** Some funds are specifically targeted at projects over a certain size. For example, most European Social Fund funding rounds require that projects should be over £10,000 in size, but in practice most projects are over £20-25,000. Other funds such as Global Grants and Awards for All are aimed at much smaller projects.

- **Timing** Some funds are always open for applications but, as mentioned above, other funds are organised into bidding rounds and you can apply only at certain times – sometimes only once a year or less. As a general rule, charitable trusts are more likely to invite open bidding, and the larger funds such as Lottery and European funds are almost always organised into rounds.

- **Your resources** Some funds require that you bring your own match funding (see above). Match funding can be brought in from other grant funding sources but the difference in timing between the different funding rounds means that there is a risk that you will have to find alternative sources of match funding to those you had planned. At the last resort, this will mean the use of your own organisational resources as match funding. For a large organisation, this kind of financial hit can be absorbed, but it could be disastrous for a smaller organisation.

■ **Your target beneficiary group** While some funds are very broad in nature, others are extremely specific about what they will support. For example the Home Office Refugee Challenge Fund will only support projects that work with refugees. The larger funds such as National Lottery and European funds are very broad in what they will fund in general, but individual funding rounds may be targeted much more specifically.

■ **What you want to pay for** Most funds will pay for salaries and running costs, but not all will pay for equipment and building work. In general, grant funding will pay only for costs that are directly related to the project, although a small number of funds will pay for the core running costs of small, voluntary organisations. Some types of costs, such as bank charges and fees to consultants for writing bids, are hardly ever eligible for grant funding. You will need to check that any match funding also follows guidelines for eligibility.

■ **How oversubscribed the fund is** Some of the larger funding schemes can seem like a good bet because such large sums of money are available. But if the ratio of bids submitted to bids successful is 50 to 1 (which can happen, especially in London) then your chances of being funded might be better with one of the smaller funds that receives fewer bids. It is worth doing some research on this, and in most cases the funding body will be able to give you an indication of the number of bids they are expecting.

■ **Other sources of support** If you are a small voluntary sector organisation, you may be eligible for support and advice that will help you to apply for funds or deliver projects more easily. This is worth bearing in mind if your organisation is relatively new to grant funding. If you are applying for or thinking of applying for European funding, help and support should be available in your local area in terms of training and advice – your local Voluntary Services Council or Learning and Skills Council should be able to help. In addition, the Neighbourhood Renewal Community Learning Chest gives training grants to community-based organisations in Neighbourhood Renewal Areas. For more information on this, see **www.neighbourhood.gov.uk/clchests.asp**

Guide to the major funds

This section will take you through some of the major sources of funding that individual organisations can apply for. It is not meant to be entirely comprehensive but will give an overview of the types and sources of funding that are out there. However, at the end of the day there is no substitute for your own research. The information and websites given in this section were correct at the time of going to press but are subject to change.

Some funds, such as Neighbourhood Renewal, are not directly available to individual organisations but are run via large partnerships. These are not included here, however information on Neighbourhood Renewal can be found at **www.neighbourhood.gov.uk**.

Funds from Europe

Four of the European Structural Funds are available in the UK:

■ **The European Regional Development Fund (ERDF)** This is only available in certain areas of the UK. It mainly supports infrastructure projects (building, improved transport etc) and support and advice for industry.

■ **The European Social Fund (ESF)** This is available everywhere and supports human resource development such as training and advice.

■ **The European Agricultural Guidance and Guarantee Fund (EAGGF)** This fund supports projects in rural areas.

■ **The Financial Instrument for Fisheries Guidance (FIFG)** This offers support for the restructuring of the fishing industry.

General information on European funds can be found on the DTI website at:

www.dti.gov.uk/europe/structural.html

ERDF can be accessed only by applying through a **local area partnership** in regions that are eligible for the funding. More details can be found on the DTI website.

Both EAGGF and FIFG are only available in the most deprived rural regions in the UK. The application process is similar to that for ERDF.

ESF, however, can be accessed a number of ways.

1 **Direct bidding** Some ESF funding can be accessed by direct

application to the Government Offices for the Regions (England), the Welsh European Funding Office, The Scottish ESF Objective 3 Partnership **(www.objective3.org)** or the European Division of the Department of Finance and Personnel (Northern Ireland). Bidding is organised into rounds with strict deadlines and is governed by regional priorities. For direct bidding, match funding will be required.

2   **Co-financing** Increasingly, ESF is now available through intermediary bodies with match funding already in place. These intermediary bodies, or **Co-Financing Organisation (CFOs)** include Learning and Skills Councils, JobCentre Plus, Connexions and Regional Development Agencies. The types of project that can be funded are usually much more restricted than with direct bidding, but there is the huge advantage of not having to find match funding.

3   **Community Initiatives** There are four community initiatives funded in the UK through a ring-fenced amount of the structural funds budget. These are usually accessed only by large partnerships, including partners from other European countries.

4   **Global Grants** Grants of up to £10,000 (with no match funding required) are available to voluntary sector organisations who work with ESF target beneficiary groups. In Scotland and Wales the grants are administered by the Scottish Council for Voluntary Organisations **(www.scvo.org.uk)** and the Wales Council for Voluntary Action **(www.wcva.org.uk)** respectively. In England, Global Grants are administered regionally and locally by intermediary bodies. A list of these bodies is available from the Government Offices in the Regions.

National Lottery

'National Lottery Good Causes' is a blanket term covering a range of grant funding schemes. Lottery funding has supported projects in sport, arts, heritage, millennium projects, charities and 'new opportunities' (health, education and the environment).

■   A range of **Sports** grants are available supporting projects that encourage more people to take part in sports. Funding is also available for small community sports groups.

■   **Arts** projects are supported through the Arts Councils. Much of the money goes to large capital projects, but individual artists and arts organisations can apply for grants to support their work and to bring arts to new audiences.

■   The **Heritage Lottery Fund** gives grants to preserve and develop historic buildings, archives, natural sites, museum collections and important industrial and transport sites for future generations.

■ The **Millennium Award Scheme** gives small grants of up to £2,000 to individuals and groups who want to make a difference in their community.

■ Charitable projects are supported via the **Community Fund**. The fund contains a number of different grant schemes aimed at projects of all sizes, and beneficiaries of these projects should be people facing the greatest disadvantage in society.

■ Finally, the **New Opportunities Fund** supports projects in health, education or the environment. Like the Community Fund, it mainly supports projects that will help the most disadvantaged.

Full information on Lottery funding and all of the strands mentioned above can be found at:

www.lotterygoodcauses.org.uk/about.htm.

There is also a helpline number that you can call for more information: 0845 275 0000.

Charitable Trusts

Grant-making charitable trusts vary enormously both in size and in intent. Some are geographically restricted, others are restricted to supporting projects working with a certain group (e.g. young people). It all depends on the aims and objectives of the trust and the decisions made by the trustees, who may be very cautious about which projects they support. However, grant-making trusts can be extremely useful sources of funding for projects with a social or charitable aim and the funding is often a lot more flexible than that given out by the larger funding bodies.

Because there are over 8,000 charitable trusts in the UK it is impossible to list them all here or even give an overview of the larger ones and so you will need to carry out your own research. A good place to start is the Association of Charitable Foundations (www.acf.org.uk; 2 Plough Yard, Shoreditch High Street, London EC2A 3LP). This not only gives information on how to locate grant-making trusts and foundations, but also contains useful information and advice for bidders.

Other regeneration funding

New funding schemes are developed on an ongoing basis and some can come and go very quickly. The following bodies often run grant-funding schemes and are well worth researching.

- **Government departments** This includes the devolved government departments in Scotland, Northern Ireland and Wales. Examples of recent funding schemes include the Home Office Refugee Challenge Fund and the Department for International Development Business Linkages Challenge Fund. Government Departments are subject to rapid and unexpected change, so you will need to ensure that any information you have is fully up to date. More funding is available on a regional or local basis. The Regional Co-ordination Unit has a list of funds available which can be found at:
  www.rcu.gov.uk/abi/default.asp

- **Regional Development Agencies** As well as working with the European Structural Funds, RDAs have their own sources of funding for regional development. Projects supported by RDAs will usually have an industry focus or will support urban or rural development.

- **Learning and Skills Councils** The LSCs in England run a number of different funding schemes including, most recently, the Local Intervention and Development Fund (LID). Information about the Learning and Skills Councils can be found at **www.lsc.gov.uk** or by phone on 0870 900 6800.

- **Sector-specific funding** Higher and Further Education organisations and schools can all bid for funding specific to their sector, for example the Higher Education Innovation Fund. Similarly, there are funds that are only available for organisations working in the areas of, for example, health or business support. Voluntary and community sector organisations can usually apply for grants from Local Authorities. All of these can be excellent sources of funding and are not necessarily linked to projects or outcomes.

Every type of funding scheme is slightly different, with different aims and objectives and different regulations. Finding a source of funding that you think will fit your project and your organisation can take time and research, but it is time well spent. The better the fit, the more likely it is that you will be successful in winning funding.

CHAPTER TWO

Developing your project idea

Planning your project

Contrary to what most people believe, good writing on a bidding form is not the most important factor in winning funding. Much more important is to have a well worked out idea for a project that is realistic, innovative and clear. Most people who have served on bid scoring panels have seen bids that are cleverly written with well researched evidence, but where it is not clear what the project will actually do! Far more convincing is a bid that is perhaps more simply written, but where the ideas behind the project shine through and are convincing in their own right.

The secret to this is good project planning before even attempting to put pen to paper on the bidding form. There is always a temptation to skip over the project planning stage, especially if time is short. However, I would advise from my own experience to fit in as much planning as you possibly can in the time available. It makes for a better bid, and the bidding form will be easier and quicker to write.

Where to start

In reality, project planning for a bid doesn't always start with a project idea. Often organisations will look at an upcoming funding round and write a bid to fit the needs of the round. This can be a good way to go about things because it means that the bid will (or should!) fit the needs of the funding round perfectly. But this approach will only work if the organisation has the skills and experience to deliver what is asked for. There is no point in chasing money for its own sake, and it is better to spend time researching other sources of funding rather than ending up with a project that you can't deliver.

Perhaps the ideal scenario would be that an organisation, with a clear idea of its own mission and objectives, is inspired by the priorities and objectives of an upcoming funding round to develop a project that meets both the requirements of the funding round and the needs and abilities of the organisation.

Think about your own organisation:

- ☐ *Can you sum up its purpose in one sentence?*

- ☐ *Who is the main client group (or groups) that your organisation works with?*

☐ *What experience have the staff had in developing and delivering projects in the past?*

☐ *Does your organisation's purpose and experience fit with the requirements of the funding round you are interested in?*

☐ *Are there other funding rounds that might be more suitable?*

If you are working through this book to write a specific bid for your organisation, pause for a moment. Do you have a basic idea of the project you want to develop, and have you found a funding round that fits it? If so, you are ready to move on.

What's the big idea?

So you've selected the fund you want to go for and have an idea of the project you want to deliver. Now is the time to start tightening up your idea and turning it into a proper project definition.

The essence of writing a project definition is to answer the questions:

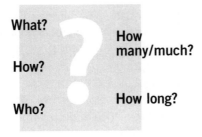

What?

How?

Who?

How many/much?

How long?

We're going to look at each of these in turn.

What?

What are you trying to do? You should be able to give a summary of your project in a short phrase – no more than one sentence. This should convey the main point or aim of your project. One way to do this is to use the format:

We will...

For example:

- ■ **We will** prepare refugees for work.
- ■ **We will** help new business to start up.
- ■ **We will** help young people who are excluded from school.

*What will you do in **your** project?*

How?

How will you achieve what you have said you will do? The statement you have made about what you are going to do will need to be qualified by a statement of how you will achieve it.

For example:

- ■ **We will** prepare refugees for work **by** providing ESOL support, advice and guidance and vocational training.
- ■ **We will** help new business to start up **by** running a business start-up training programme for entrepreneurs and providing incubator space.
- ■ **We will** help young people who are excluded from school **by** running a volunteer placement scheme in care homes and a programme of self-development and life skills.

*How will you achieve **your** project?*

Who?

You may have already partly answered this question because you should have at least some idea of who the project is aimed at. In the first example above, the team developing the project have identified **refugees** as the target group. However, 'refugees' is a very broad group encompassing hundreds of thousands of people. The team needs to narrow it down a little.

In this example, the team might decide to target:

Refugees...

    ...living in Luton...

        ...who have been granted
        refugee status less than a
        year ago.

Alternatively they might have decided to target:

Refugees...

    ...in the South of England...

        ...from Somalia.

Either of these would give a much greater focus to the project.

*Who will **you** be targeting?*

Another aspect to working out the answer to 'who' is to start thinking about other organisations that might be involved with the project. You may already know the answer to this – there may be partners that you already work with or services you would like to include in the project but know you can't deliver alone. This is something you can think about in more detail when you start to put the project plan together.

How many/much?

This is the point at which you start to look at the size of your proposed project. How much do you want to achieve? What do you think is achievable? At this point there may be a little bit of guesswork involved. That doesn't matter, because right now you are just trying to get an initial idea of your project together. It can all be refined and changed as your idea develops.

The way you answer this question will depend on the kind of project you have in mind. For example, you might want to think about the number of people you will help, or in the case of a building project, the size of the building:

■ We will prepare *150* refugees for work...

- We will provide incubator space for *10* start-up businesses
- We will help *10* young people who are excluded from school

If your project involves research, you might instead like to think about how many people you will survey, for example.

*How will you answer this question for **your** project?*

How long?

The length of your project may not be an entirely free choice. Some funds have a set period of time in which the money has to be spent (for example, the European Social Fund). Others will have a maximum length of project (such as two years). It will be up to you when you start and finish your project within these limits. Most people will try to go for the maximum length of time possible, and while this is understandable it is not always the best decision. Sometimes it is wiser to finish the project a month or so before the end date set by the funding agency – so that if you do happen to over-run or take longer than you expect to achieve the outcomes then there will be room for negotiation. It is virtually impossible to get an extension beyond the cut-off date set by the funding agency, especially in the case of European funds.

*What will be the start and end date of **your** project?*

Aims and objectives

If you have worked through the exercises above, you have just written the **aims** and **objectives** for your project.

An **aim** is a general statement of what the project will achieve. You wrote the aim for your project when you answered the questions What? How? and Who?

Objectives are more detailed statements about what will be achieved by the project. You started to write objectives for your project by answering How Many/Much? and How Long? Basically, objectives say 'our project will do these things'. In the example above, one project has the objective:

■ We will help 10 young people who are excluded from school

This states the overall achievement of the project. The project team might want to write some more objectives describing some of the other achievements along the way. For example:

■ We will provide a 16 week structured programme of learning for the young people on the project

■ 5 young people will achieve a qualification

■ 6 young people will return to mainstream schooling

Some books, and some bidding documents, talk about **SMART** Objectives. SMART stands for:

Specific

– You are clear about exactly what will be achieved.

Measurable

– You are able to tell when the objective has been achieved.

Achievable

– It is possible to achieve the objective within the lifetime of the project and with the resources available.

Realistic

– You are sure the objectives could be achieved (for example, you have done similar projects before, or know an organisation that has).

Time bound

– There is a time limit or an 'achieve by' date set for each objective.

Let's look at one of the example objectives above and see if it is SMART.

■ We will provide a 16 week structured programme of learning for the young people on the project

This is **Specific** because it clearly states what will be done.

It is **Measurable** because at the end of the 16 week programme of learning you could say 'we have now achieved this objective'.

Whether or not it is **Achievable** depends on the organisation that is running the project. Do they have enough expertise to run the learning programme, and have they bid for enough money to cover the costs? If so, this objective is probably achievable.

The objective seems to be **Realistic** because other organisations have put on learning programmes for excluded young people before. In other words it can be done, it's not just pie in the sky!

However, this objective is not yet **Time bound** as there is no information about when this will take place. It could easily be rewritten to include this information. For example:

- We will provide a 16-week structured programme of learning for the young people on the project *between 1 September 2002 and 31 March 2003*

OR

- We will provide a 16-week structured programme of learning for the young people on the project *that will be completed by 31 March 2003*

This information about time also makes the objective more measurable because by 31 March, the organisation will know whether or not they managed to achieve their objective.

Make a list of about 3 – 5 objectives for your project. Are they SMART?

At this stage, you are still getting your ideas together. Your aim and objectives might change slightly as you go on to develop the project further. In fact it is quite common for changes to be made once you start working out the costs for the project.

Project scope

The next step towards defining your project is working out its **scope**. The scope of a project is a statement of what it will and will not deliver. This can be a good way of moving from your initial idea to something more concrete. Scoping can be done as a series of statements covering what you will and won't do. For example:

- We will provide each beneficiary with 40 hours training over 5 weeks
- We will not provide work placements
- We will not provide counselling
- We will provide advice and guidance

What are the scoping statements for your project?

What will it take?

Now you have a much clearer idea of your project – but can you achieve it? If your project is the same as or similar to something you have already done in the past, you may want to skip this section. If not, this is where you abandon all optimism and take a long hard look at your project, your team, your organisation and your partners!

First of all you need to break the project down into smaller steps. There are various ways of doing this, but perhaps the easiest is to start with your list of objectives and work out how each of them can be achieved.

Taking our example from above:

■ We will provide a 16-week structured programme of learning for the young people on the project *between 1 September 2002 and 31 March 2003*

What would need to be done to make this happen?

If this was your project, you might start by making a rough list of things that would need to be done – a list of project **tasks**. For example:

■ Plan the curriculum

■ Assign tutors

■ Find placements in care homes

■ Buy books and other teaching materials

■ Draw up the timetable

■ Teach the course

■ Progress reviews every 4 weeks

Some of these would need a bit more thought, for example 'find placements in care homes' might involve checking your insurance to see if you are covered for any accident that might happen to one of the young people while on placement, and carrying out health and safety assessments on the homes.

Go through your list of objectives and list all the tasks that need to be done to achieve each one. You do not have to go into too much detail at this stage.

There will also be tasks that need to be done that are not directly linked to any of the objectives. These might include:

- Recruiting beneficiaries to the project
- Project management
- Setting up a steering group
- Managing project finances
- Recruiting new staff

*What other tasks will you have to carry out to achieve **your** project?*

By now you should have a list of tasks, and perhaps a clearer idea of what needs to be done to carry out your project. Sometimes it can come as a surprise just how much there is to do, especially if you are new to running projects. This list of tasks is important because from it, you can start to plan out how long it will take you to carry out the project, how much it might cost, how many staff are needed and what skills and experience those staff will need to have.

How long will it take?

You may already know how long your project will take, as it may be tied to other timescales such as the length of the funding period, or an academic year. If so, you might want to skip over to the next section. If not, this section will help you to put together an outline project schedule to estimate how long individual tasks and the whole project will take to complete. A project **schedule** is a graphical representation of a project and its tasks, plotted against time.

The first stage is to estimate how long each individual task will take – the task **duration**. For a task such as 'teach a 16-week course' the duration is obvious – 16 weeks! For other tasks such as 'plan the curriculum' or 'recruit beneficiaries' it is less obvious, and you will have to find a way to estimate the duration.

There are many ways to estimate task duration. You could rely on your own or someone else's experience from similar projects, or ask the person or organisation who will be carrying out the task. **Beware of optimists!** Some people will always underestimate how long tasks take to complete, which means that when the project is underway nothing will be completed on time. If in doubt, ask more than one person for an estimate and go with the average.

Sometimes it is appropriate to split tasks into smaller tasks in order to get an accurate estimate. For example, the task:

■ Recruit beneficiaries to the project

might be broken down into smaller tasks such as:

■ Develop database of potential beneficiaries

■ Write text for leaflet

■ Design leaflet

■ Proof read leaflet

■ Print leaflet

■ Mail leaflet out to database

■ Drop copies of the leaflet at all local community centres

Once you break a task down like this, it becomes much easier to work out how long it might take. For example, the durations for the list of tasks above might look something like this:

Task no	Task	Duration
1	Develop database of potential beneficiaries	5 days
2	Write text for leaflet	1 day
3	Design leaflet	1 day
4	Proof read leaflet	1 day
5	Print leaflet	3 days
6	Mail leaflet out to database	2 days
7	Drop copies of the leaflet at all local community centres	3 days
	TOTAL	**16 days**

Table 1

If the same person were to do all of the tasks on the list, it would take at least 16 working days to carry out the overall activity 'recruit beneficiaries to the project' – more than three weeks! Unless the project team was very experienced at carrying out similar projects, they could easily have underestimated how long this would take.

A chart of the tasks would look like this:

Activity: Recruit beneficiaries

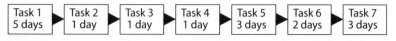

Figure 1

However, more than one person may be involved in carrying out these tasks. For example, task 1 might be carried out by the marketing manager whereas tasks 2-4 might be carried out by the project manager. What's more, the first task of developing the database can continue while the leaflet is being printed. The database is only really needed in time for task 6, the mailout, to begin. This means that task 1 can be carried out at the same time as tasks 2-5, reducing the time it will take to carry out the overall activity.

The first part of the chart would now look like this:

Activity: Recruit beneficiaries

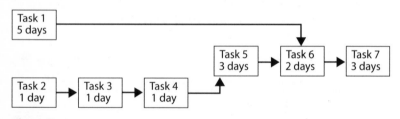

Figure 2

The whole series of tasks now takes only 11 days.

Task 5, 'print the leaflet', has been estimated as 3 days, based on how long it will take the printers to physically print and send back the leaflet. But what if the printers had a backlog of work and couldn't start the print job straight away? If the waiting time is estimated as 4 days, the chart will now look like this:

Activity: Recruit beneficiaries

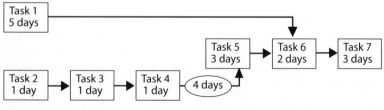

Figure 3

In Figure 3, the quickest the activity could be done is now 15 days because of the waiting time.

If you want to develop a timetable for project tasks, you could now start adding real dates to the diagram to take into account weekends and other holiday times. The first part of the diagram would look something like this:

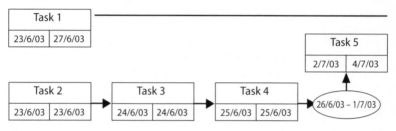

Figure 4

This sort of diagram is known as a **PERT chart**. The date on the left is the start date of the task and the finish date is given on the right. As you can see in Figure 4, weekends have been taken into account. This can be used to give a start and end date to different parts of the project, or to the whole project. It can also be used to work out the date of milestones.

Milestones are events or achievements that happen during the course of the project, with a date, that can be used to ensure it is on track. For example, '10 beneficiaries recruited' could be a milestone and a PERT chart like the one above can be used to work out a realistic date by which this milestone can be reached – e.g. '10 beneficiaries recruited by 31 July 2003'. Funding bodies often want to see a project plan that includes a list of milestones. Careful planning will ensure that you come up with a realistic set of milestones that you are confident of achieving.

*Work out the duration of each of the tasks in **your** project.*

How do the tasks interlink?

How long will it take to complete the whole project?

Project planning is not a simple, straightforward task and in working out the timescales for your project you may need to consider at the same time who is available to carry out each of the tasks.

Who will do what?

For each task, it is important to work out the **skills** and **qualifications** needed to carry out the task. This will help you to make sure that each task is carried out by the right person. For example, teaching on a course might require someone who has a teaching qualification. Sometimes the skills needed for a task are less obvious, for example negotiation skills might be needed for the task of convening a steering group.

At this stage, don't worry about whether or not your team has the right skills or qualifications but concentrate on the tasks themselves. The information can be summarised in a table such as the one below:

Task	Skills/qualifications needed

Table 2

Fill in this table for all the tasks in your project.

Now you can start to look at the actual people who will carry out the project. This might include people from within your organisation, people from partner organisations, new recruits or consultants/experts.

For each of the tasks in the table above, you can add the name of a person (or a partner organisation) who has the required skills and qualifications listed, or who can achieve the skills and qualifications through training. Where you will need to recruit a new employee or a consultant, you can write this down instead of naming an actual person or organisation. You can summarise this information by adding an extra column to the table above. An example of how this table might look for our example project is shown opposite:

Task	Skills/qualifications needed	Name
Plan the curriculum	Background in education Planning skills Knowledge of key stage 4	1 Carole Khan 2 Expert advisor from the Local Education Authority
Find suitable placements	Negotiation skills Some health and safety awareness	Connie Bootham (project manager) – **will need to go on a health and safety course**
Teach the course	Teaching qualification 2 specialists in life skills 1 specialist in care/social work	Three teachers needed 1 Yasmin Carter 2 Thomas Weiss 3 Someone from 'Community Care' (partner organisation)
Progress reviews	Tutorial and counselling skills	Part time tutor/counsellor (new recruit)
etc.		

Table 3

As you can see, some tasks need more than one person to be involved. As you go through and add names to the tasks, you may realise that there are tasks you have missed out from the list, or that some people will need extra training. This doesn't matter, because you can change things and add things as you go along – in fact this is why the project planning stage is needed!

If you need to recruit extra staff, or to buy in consultants from outside, the list of skills/qualifications should help you to draw up a good job description.

Complete table 3 for your project.

- *How many people will be involved in delivering the project?*

- *Are they all available?*

- *Have all partner organisations agreed to take part?*

- *Do any of the staff require further training? (Some funds will allow you to bid for money for staff training.)*

- *Will you need to recruit any further staff or consultants?*

Costing the project

The next step is to cost up the whole project and create a **budget**. Knowing how long each task will last, and the timescales for the project overall, will help here. It is also helpful to know who will be carrying out project tasks, as there might be extra costs associated with recruiting new staff, or you may be able to get rates for specific consultants and experts that you know you will need.

Project costs fall into a number of categories. One of the main distinctions is between **capital** and **revenue** costs. Capital costs relate to building projects or the purchase of major items of equipment. Capital funding tends to represent a long term investment of funding into an area. On the other hand, revenue costs are the day to day running costs of a project, for example salaries and rent. Some funds (for example the European Social Fund) will fund only revenue costs for projects and will not pay for items of equipment that are over a certain cost. It is always worth checking before you write the bid that the fund you are applying to will cover the kind of costs that you are going to incur.

Types of revenue costs

Staff costs

Staff costs relate to the cost of salaries and on-costs (for example, pension contributions, national insurance) for staff working on the project. Some funding bodies may also fund staff training and staff travel.

Usually, only the time that staff actually spend working on project activities can be paid for by the grant. In some cases this will be the person's whole salary, but in other cases only a proportion of the salary can be claimed. If an individual has been specifically hired to work just on the one project then you can safely claim their whole salary. However, people working on more than one project will have to find a way to account for the time they spend on each project, for instance by completing **time sheets** to show how they are spending their working time.

Beneficiary costs

In the case of many funds, you can ask for money to help beneficiaries access the project more easily. For example, you can budget for payments towards travel or childcare costs for beneficiaries.

Other costs

Other costs include rent of premises, bills such as electricity and telephones, leasing costs, administrative costs, legal and accountancy services, items of stationery, software and small items of equipment. If a building and its resources are used for more than one project, a method needs to be found to apportion the costs of running the building fairly across the different projects. Different funders will have different rules as to how this should be done.

Estimating costs

How much the project will cost depends on a number of factors:

- How long the project will last

- How many beneficiaries the project will support

- Salaries of the staff involved

- Whether any specialist equipment is required

- Whether or not the project includes spend on capital items

- How much match funding is available (if applicable)

When you first estimate the costs for a project, you should include any match funding contributions as well, so that you can work out the total cost of the project. Some of the things you will need to think about include:

- Whether you will cost the project on a monthly, quarterly or annual basis. This will depend on how the bidding form asks for the information. For your own monitoring purposes you may want to convert the budget into a monthly table of costs at a later date

- How many staff you will need, and whether they will be full time or part time

- Whether project partners will want to be paid for the work they do, or whether they are bringing match funding

- What support the beneficiaries of the project will need and how much this will cost

- Whether your project will need to commission an external audit or evaluation, and how much this will cost

- What it will cost, in terms of staff time, to administer the funds and to meet the requirements of the funding bodies for monitoring and record keeping

Some of the cost categories that you might want to include are set out in table 4 below. This example is based on a revenue-only project.

Cost category	Quarter 1 Year 1	Quarter 2 Year 2
Staff Costs Project Manager (full time) Project Administrator (part time – 60%) Monitoring Officer (part time – 10%) Support Worker (full time) Trainer (full time) Learning Support (part time – 30%) Cleaner (hourly rate) Project Evaluator (to contract)		
Beneficiary Costs		
Travel costs (£X per day x 30 days x 10 beneficiaries) Childcare costs (£X per day x 30 days x 2 beneficiaries) Subsistence (30 lunches x £X)		
Other Costs		
Rent and rates Telephone Utilities Training materials Stationery and consumables Marketing and publicity Insurance Computer software Audit fees		

Table 4: Example Project Budget

The above is just an example and may contain cost categories that are not eligible under some funding schemes. However, it should give you a starting point from which to think about the cost categories for your own project.

*What are the cost categories for **your** project?*

What are the costs associated with these categories?

Are all these costs eligible under the funding scheme you are applying for?

When you have worked out the initial costings for your project, you may find that it costs a lot more than you originally thought – this is by no means unusual! While it is important to be realistic about what it will cost to deliver the project, you have to balance this with being realistic about how much money the funders will give you. This can be a tricky balancing act and you will have to ask yourself difficult questions and possibly think of alternative ways to deliver the project that will use up less staff time and resources.

Putting together the project plan

A project plan should consist of:

- The aims and objectives of the project
- A scoping statement
- A project schedule with milestones
- A list of who will work on the project and how their skills, qualifications and experience fit the project tasks – with a note of any training needs
- A project budget

Once you have a completed project plan, you are ready to move on to the next chapter and write the bid.

CHAPTER THREE

Tackling
the form

The form

Different funding bodies require different levels of information about your project, ranging from a simple 1 or 2-page expression of interest to a 40-page form. You may be asked to describe your organisation as well as your project. In some cases you may have to justify how your project fits with the aims, objectives or priorities of the funding body, and give evidence as to why the project is needed in that particular area or for that particular group of beneficiaries.

Before you start writing

One of the main things you need to do before you write the bid is to plan the project, and that was the subject of the last chapter. Next you'll need to read all the documents about the funding issued by the funding body. These might include:

- Funding prospectus
- Scoring or assessment criteria
- List of funding priorities
- Strategic documents produced by the funding body

It is vitally important that you read through all of these documents in some detail and become familiar with them before you start to draft the bid. This will ensure that you address the issues that are important to the funders in your answers.

You will also need to carry out some background research to support your project bid. This could include:

- Reports and research on your beneficiary group
- Local area information
- Information about other projects in the area

You will need to look for statistics and quotations that support the case you are making for your project. For example, if you say that your project is needed because lone parents find it difficult to access work because their skills are out of date, you should be able to find some kind of evidence to back this up. Examples of how to do this are given later in this chapter.

Answering questions – an overview

Bidding forms vary from fund to fund. ERDF forms are different from SRB which are different in turn from Lottery. However, most forms tend to ask the same kind of questions in order to establish some basic facts about the proposed project and to allow it to be judged in either a competitive or a strategic way (or some combination of the two).

Questions will normally fall into one of the following categories:

? Basic factual questions

Examples:

> What is the name of the project?
>
> Legal status of lead organisation?

How to answer:

These will be the most straightforward of all the questions to answer as long as you have a clear idea of the project and the organisations that will be involved in its delivery.

Points to look out for:

Some forms will require a lot of information about the lead organisation and in fact may rule out certain organisations from leading a project. For example, organisations may have to be part of an approved list, or may need to demonstrate 3 years of accounts before being allowed to take part in the bidding round. Certain types of organisations may be ruled out altogether, for example private sector companies or very small community-based groups. In some cases, only organisations based in a particular geographic area may be able to bid. It is always worth checking at an early stage whether your organisation is eligible to bid. If not, you could consider asking a partner organisation to lead the bid. It is also worth double-checking at this stage that the proposed project fits in with the objectives and values of your organisation, and that it has management support (preferably in writing).

? Questions about the project

Examples:

> Give a brief summary of the project in no more than 100 words.
>
> How will the project be delivered?

How to answer:

The key to answering this type of question is to be very clear and concise. You do not need to write in complex, technical language in order to score highly. In actual fact this makes the bid very difficult to understand for a scorer who may be asked to assess many bids during the course of a day. So keep it simple.

The clearer you are about the project and what you are trying to achieve, the better you will be able to convey it in the bid.

Points to look out for:

Some forms will ask for information about a project over the course of several questions. Make sure that you read each question carefully and only include information about the specific aspect that is being asked about – otherwise you will end up repeating yourself.

? Justification questions

Examples:

> How does the project fit in with the priority and measure of the funding round?
>
> What is the need for the project within the region?
>
> Show how your project meets the needs of the targeted beneficiary group.

How to answer:

These questions will tend to take a little more time to answer, and research is the key.

Questions about **fit with the funding** round can be answered by gathering as much information as possible about the fund – including not only the guidance provided but any background and strategic documents.

Questions about **regional (or sector-based)** need should be answered based on strategies and reports available from, for example, Learning and Skills Councils, Government Offices and Regional Development Agencies. Many of these are now available on the web. Questions about **beneficiary needs** can be based on experience and feedback from other projects, regional or national research into the particular groups, or a combination of the two. A good starting point can be the background documents for the funding programme. When they are first set up, most major funding programmes have to justify why they are aimed at certain groups, and this justification is based on commissioned research.

Quality is far better than quantity in answering these questions, and two or three good sources of information clearly explained are better than two pages of quotes and references. See the examples in Chapter 3 for more information.

Points to look out for:

Don't assume that the person scoring the bid will be familiar with the research sources you use, or even the fine details of the funding guidance. It is up to you to explain exactly what needs or aims your project meets and how it meets them. Always reference your sources clearly. Don't just provide quotes or statistics, explain them in the context of your project.

? Statistical questions

Examples:

> Age, gender and ethnic breakdowns of beneficiaries.
>
> From which business sectors are the companies you will be helping drawn?

How to answer:

There is really no substitute for experience in gauging the sort of beneficiaries you are likely to attract to a project. You will need to have a very clear idea of how specific groups are to be targeted and recruited, and be realistic about your chances of attracting the profile of beneficiaries that you state in the bid.

If your organisation has experience in working with the targeted group you should mention this, being as specific as possible about the projects or activities you have been involved in and the successes you achieved.

Points to look out for:

In the past there has been a tendency to answer these questions based on beneficiary groups that will gain the bid a higher score – for example homeless people or refugees. Many organisations have since found that they do not have the experience to attract people from these groups onto their project. Although it is usually possible to make changes to a project once it has started, change in beneficiary profile can have an overall impact on the funding programme as a whole and may not be allowed. In the worst case, the project may be asked to return money or prevented from making further claims.

Therefore, it is worth being as realistic as possible when profiling beneficiaries on the bidding form. If you don't have experience in working with the particular group targeted in your project, you should think about how you are going to attract them and work with them. For example, you could work in partnership with an organisation that does have the specialist experience of working with that group.

? Financial questions

Examples:

> Please provide a breakdown of project costs under the following headings...
>
> State the amount and source of match funding.
>
> What is the unit cost per output?

How to answer these questions:

You will need to carry out a full project costing exercise before attempting to answer these questions. Further information about project costing can be found in Chapter 2.

Points to look out for:

If the project requires match funding and this is not confirmed, this represents a risk to your organisation. If your organisation has a policy on match funding (and if not, it is certainly recommended that it should) then you will need to ensure that you are acting in line with this. It is also worth being aware that while the amount of funding awarded to a project may go down, it practically never goes up, so if you have omitted any items of expenditure at this stage you may not be able to recoup them later.

Tackling the form

The key to answering question on the form well is to keep it simple and answer the question you are asked. This will involve not just reading the question, but looking at any scoring criteria you have been given, as these give you hints on the sort of answer the scorer is looking for. For example a Regional Development Agency recently ran a bidding round, and the form included a box that looked like this:

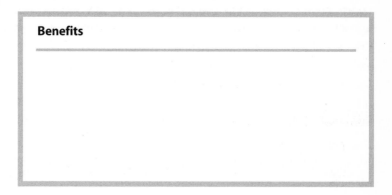

Here, the funders are clearly looking for some information about the benefits of the project. However, what they were looking for was far more specific than that. The scoring framework document had this to say:

> Benefits – what are the long term benefits to the RDA of your project and how will your project achieve these, refer to the tier two outcomes and tier three outputs in the RDA Corporate Plan.

So in order to answer this question, you would have to read the RDA Corporate Plan and refer to how your project meets the outputs given in the Plan, rather than just talking about the overall benefits of your project. This sounds obvious, but it is surprising how many people do not read the guidance notes or scoring criteria properly and therefore get a low score because they don't give the required information.

On the other hand, it is not enough simply to quote the right documents. You will need to put these in the context of your project – use the information to justify what you want to do and how you want to do it. This is a lot easier if you have gone through a project planning process, because your project idea will be much better thought out.

The 'Web Support' project bid

The rest of this chapter will use a real-life bid that was funded by a Regional Development Agency (RDA) as an example of how to answer the different kinds of question. The bid has been slightly amended so that the organisations involved can remain anonymous. We will call the organisation who submitted the bid 'ProTraining'.

Although the bid was funded, it did not score full marks and is by no means perfect. However, as one bid writer said, 'good enough is good enough'. You do not have to write the perfect bid in order to win funding, just one that is good enough to score highly, or to persuade a panel to fund the project.

This bid may be very different from the kind of project you are working on, but the principles of good bid writing are the same. Footnotes will be used throughout this chapter to highlight specific points about the bid and what the bid writer was attempting to show.

At the end of this chapter, extracts will be given from a range of other bidding forms with comments about how the questions can be tackled.

The 'Web Support' project was set up by ProTraining to provide Information and Communication Technology (ICT) help and support for small businesses by training their employees in web design. It also offered technology audits for the businesses themselves, and each beneficiary was expected to work on a web project that would help their business, with the support of tutors on the project. It was funded by the RDA as part of an ESF Co-financing bidding round.

The project within the regional and strategic context

The first question on the form was 'Demonstrate the strategic and geographic fit for the project'. Questions like this can often be found on bidding forms. They allow the bid writer to show how the individual project fits in with the bigger picture, and how it will help to bring about the overall vision of the funding body. At the end of the day, every funding body has its own particular agenda and set of interests. These are usually set out in some kind of document such as a strategic plan. If you can convince the funders that your project helps them to achieve their aims, you are far more likely to be funded.

Similarly, if there are plans for the local area or region you may be asked to show how your project fits in with these. All Local Authorities now have to produce a Community Plan, and many have a Neighbourhood Renewal Strategy. These documents are freely available either on the web or by getting directly in touch with the Local Authority. By showing that your project fits in with these plans, you can show that your project is helping to meet the needs of the area and is co-ordinated with the work of other organisations.

The scoring framework had this to say about the question:

> *Describe how the project meets and/or links to RDA priorities and strategies, and identify a clear link between the project and the geographical area it is targeting. Use relevant research or evidence to demonstrate that the geographical coverage of your project matches need. All projects must demonstrate a focus on achieving a Healthy Regional Labour Market.*

Breaking this down into different points, it shows that the scorers of the bid will be looking for:

a   links to RDA priorities and strategies

b   link between the project and its geographical area

c   use of relevant research to demonstrate that the geographical coverage of the project matches need

d   focus on a Healthy Regional Labour Market.

These form the **criteria** against which the bid will be scored. Breaking down the scoring criteria like this can be a good way to start drafting an answer to a question, because it allows you to focus on the different points you will need to cover in your answer. Clearly, there is some research to be done on the priorities and strategies of the RDA, the Healthy Regional Labour Market and the geographic area before answering this question.

1a Demonstrate the strategic and geographic fit for the project[1]
(10 points, max 1 page) [2]

Link to RDA priorities and strategies[3]
This project meets the priorities set out in the RDA funding prospectus 2003-4[4]: 'activity will focus on developing higher-level skills, in particular higher level ICT training to up-skill existing

workers'[5] (p21)[6] by providing an opportunity for key employees from small businesses to upgrade their ICT skills at a higher level, specifically in the area of web design[7].

The Regional Economic Development Strategy (2002)[8] states that: 'ICT skills shortages and a lack of e-business appreciation are key inhibitors to success. The region's workforce needs to extend its ICT knowledge' (p48)[9]. This project will meet this need by offering ICT web-enabling skills at a higher level to small business employees.

The Regional FRESA (October 2002) highlights ICT skills as a major area of skills shortage that has been consistently identified by employers (p15). This project meets two of the priorities within Strategic Objective 3, namely 'ensure that the workforce is equipped with the higher level skills required by the region's employers' and 'recognise and address the unique barriers to workforce development faced by small, medium and micro enterprises'. It will do this by providing professional, higher level ICT skills training at a location and time best suited to small business employees.

This project supports the concept of a healthy labour market[10] primarily by addressing skills needs of the workforce. As such, it will work to promote a strong supply side by helping to minimise skills gaps in the labour force in tandem with current and future employment growth[11] by concentrating on web design skills which are increasingly in demand internally as more and more small businesses develop a dynamic online presence. With reference to the diagram on page 9 of the Regional FRESA this project fits with 'investing in workforce skills'.

Geographical coverage[12]

This project is regional and will recruit from every area of the Region. The project's location adjacent to Blankville station is especially well placed for beneficiaries in North, East and Central parts of the region, with excellent public transport links[13].

The BuyIT research project (2001, Local Authority Pathfinder Project) surveyed the region's small businesses and found that 90% of small businesses in the area have a web connection and 66% wanted to make more of e-business opportunities, but that one of the perceived barriers is lack of relevant ICT skills[14]. This project will address these needs of the region's small businesses by providing an integrated package of web design training that will allow employees of small businesses to make the move to e-trading using internal staff resources. Furthermore, it will provide mentoring, advice and technical audits to the small businesses from which the individual beneficiaries are drawn, thus increasing the capacity of small businesses to utilise the technologies to which they already have access.[15]

notes

1   This is the question as it originally appeared on the form. The scoring criteria were not included with the question but were in a separate document attached to the form.

2   Bidding forms often specify a maximum length, either for each question or for the total bid. If you go over the space restriction, there is a chance that your bid will lose marks. Sometimes the maximum score for the question is given as a guide.

3   Here, the question combines two different aspects – links to RDA priorities (strategic fit) and geographic fit. Subheadings have been used by the bid writer to make it clear to the scorer which sections of the answer relate to which part of the question.

4   The writer has started by pointing out which of the priorities in the funding prospectus is being addressed by the project. This is important, because any funding bid has to meet the priorities of the funding body or it is unlikely to be successful.

5   The writer quotes the relevant sentence from the funding prospectus...

6   ...and gives the page number.

7   Most importantly, the writer describes how the project meets the priority quoted from the prospectus by stating what the project is going to do in a way that demonstrates that it meets the priority. Notice how the writer has used the same words in this second part of the sentence as the RDA used in their prospectus. The terms 'ICT' (information and communications technology) and 'higher level' were both repeated. Using similar language to that used by the funding body can be a good method of persuasion!

8   The writer is now beginning to quote from the RDA's published strategies, and therefore is addressing point (a) of the scoring criteria. The full reference for this document (including authors, and month and year of publication), was given as a footnote.

9   Again, a short quote has been given with a page reference. Notice how this and the rest of the quotations in this paragraph are embedded within sentences and how they are followed by a short explanation of how the project meets the need or requirement that the quote describes. A mistake some bid writers make is to provide lengthy quotes from relevant documents, but to forget to put them in context or explain why the quotes are relevant to the project.

10 This paragraph addresses point (d) of the scoring criteria.

11 The first part of this sentence uses words and phrases found in the key source document about the Healthy Labour Market – the Regional FRESA (Framework for Regional Skills and Employment Action).

12 Some of the details in this section of the answer have been changed to preserve the anonymity of the bid. The original answer was more detailed in terms of geography.

13 The original version of this answer specified particular areas that the bid writer knew that the RDA had prioritised for regeneration and showed how the project would be accessible to beneficiaries from these areas. This addressed point (b) of the scoring criteria.

14 By quoting evidence from a research report that covers the region in which the project was run, the bid writer is showing that there is a need for the services provided by this project within the geographic area. This addresses point (c) of the scoring criteria.

15 In these last two sentences, the bid writer is pointing out exactly how the project will address the need identified in the research report.

Notice how the writer has managed to address all the parts of the scoring criteria within the answer. It is not enough to address just one of the parts, even if you address it very well. Sometimes answers that don't attempt to address **all** parts of the scoring criteria will score nothing at all!

Cross-cutting themes

The next question is about **added value** and **innovation**. Sometimes, bidding forms will contain questions that look a little out of place or don't immediately make sense. This usually means that they are concentrating on some specific **cross-cutting themes** that the funding body has decided are important in the bidding round. In this case, you may need to do some background reading to understand what the funders (and the scorers) have in mind. Other themes that are often found in bidding forms include sustainability or sustainable development, equal opportunities, use of information technology (even in non-technical projects) and value for money. There is usually a strategic or political reason for including questions on these themes within a bidding form. For example, the European Union has a strong policy on sustainable development, and wants to ensure that all projects funded from a European source contribute to sustainability. In order to answer a question about sustainable development, you would need to read up on the EU definition of sustainable development.

In this example, the themes are 'added value' and 'innovation'. Innovation often finds its way into bid questions, because funders are keen to fund projects and activities that are new and different, rather than putting money into projects that have been run before, perhaps for many years. This is down to funders wanting to make the maximum impact on their target beneficiary groups. After all, a project that has been plodding along year in and year out without any changes is probably not setting the world on fire! What is more, it looks suspiciously like a core service – something that is always going to be needed and perhaps should be paid for by the local authority or some other

Government core funding. At the end of the day, most funders would like to fund a ground-breaking, dramatic project that would generate a lot of publicity for themselves and the fund they manage, and so asking about innovation is a way of finding out if a project is different, interesting and with high potential.

Added value is also very important to funders. They want to know that the project will add something to activities that are already being funded and that it won't duplicate activities that are already taking place. If your organisation already receives funding for projects and activities that are similar to the ones described in your bid, you may have to make a case as to why this additional funding is needed, and what it will pay for. Similarly, if there is already a lot of funded activity in your area you will need to show that your project offers different services and activities from those that are already available, and that it is complementary.

Let's have a look at how the bid writer handled these questions. The scoring criteria were:

Describe how the project will add value to what is already in place for the target group. Outline any elements of the project that are innovative or creative, including where a method of delivery is being tried in a location or with a particular target group for the first time.

Explain how the project adds value and uses innovation

Added value

This project will add value to existing provision throughout the catchment area[16]. There are already projects throughout the Region that are designed to assist small businesses to take part in e-business activities, including e-procurement. However, many of these are capital and infrastructure projects which address the hardware needs (including broadband capability) and produce bespoke or off-the-peg e-trading solutions. Examples include the European funded Blanktown broadband project (2001-2003) and the Whyville e-procurement project (2000-2002)[17]. This project will add value to these infrastructure projects by helping small businesses to develop the internal skills to build and maintain good websites that can be customised and can integrate with the e-trading solutions provided by these other projects[18]. Furthermore, this project will act as a referral point to small businesses to refer them for further help and support from other projects and services in the region[19].

Innovation

An innovative aspect of this project is that each beneficiary, as well as receiving instructional training on various aspects of web design, will be helped to select a web design project that they will work on with the support of their tutor. This project will be related to their work and will address a genuine business need for their employer (e.g. the redesign and updating of the company website)[20]. Thus the employer will be able to gain a return on the invested time during the life of the project[21]. The project work will call upon the methodologies of work based learning, enabling the beneficiaries to extend their learning into the workplace. This method of delivery has been initially piloted through ProTraining's 'Small Business Managers' ESF project, where it has been very successful, but to date has not been used in an ICT project like this[22].

It also builds on ProTraining's 'Small Business Skills' project which provided skills audits for small businesses in the region. This project will take some of the methodologies that have been developed through the skills audits and apply them for the first time to ICT by offering ICT skills and technology audits with advice and guidance for key employees within small businesses to help them to make the most of their technology.

Finally, this project is innovative in its flexibility. Small businesses will be able to nominate beneficiaries to attend different aspects of the training, mentoring and support on offer so as to develop a mix of skills within their organisation that meet their business needs[23].

notes

16   Sometimes it's a good idea to start off by saying positively that your project does meet the criteria. However, you will have to back this up with some kind of example or evidence.

17   This shows that the project team is aware of other projects in the region.

18   The bid writer is showing that this project will offer services that are missing from the other projects, and that will actually help the other projects to achieve more.

19   The project team is going to work closely with other projects and partners in the region. However, when it comes to delivering the project, the team should ensure that they do actually make referrals as they said they would.

20   The bid writer starts by pointing out an innovative feature of the project.

21 The writer points out the benefits of the project for small business employers. This is important because one of the overall aims of this bidding round was to support small businesses. So the bid writer is referring to the general aims of the bidding round and the funding body as well as addressing the specific scoring criteria for the question.

22 One way to show that a project is innovative is to show it takes good practice from another area and applies it to something new. In this sentence and the next one, ProTraining is showing that it has learned from its previously funded projects and is taking forward the good practice that it has developed. This is reassuring for funders as it demonstrates that any funding the organisation receives is likely to have a lasting impact.

23 Notice how the bid writer includes a lot of detail about the actual project and what the project will deliver. It's easy to get so caught up in meeting the scoring criteria that you forget to describe the project clearly.

As mentioned above, Equal Opportunities (or Diversity) is a common cross-cutting theme that appears frequently in bidding forms. However, it is not enough to say that your organisation has an Equal Opportunities policy. For the purposes of most bidding forms you will have to describe in some detail how the policy will be implemented in the context of this particular project. This helps the scoring panel to assess how well the project team understands the underlying issues of equality of opportunity and diversity and whether they can turn policy into practice. You may, therefore, be asked how your project will impact on particular groups in society, or how it will positively help to overcome discrimination and social exclusion within the wider community.

The question in the following example tackles the issue of Equal Opportunities from both of these angles. The scoring criteria were:

- Outline how your project will impact on: men and women, ethnic minorities, disabled people, other excluded groups.

- Describe specific elements of your project which encourage equal opportunities in the training environment and amongst employers

Explain how you will implement your Equal Opportunities policy and how this will impact on your staff and beneficiaries throughout your project. Explain how the project will positively promote and encourage equal opportunities.

Implementing Equal Opportunities

ProTraining has a comprehensive Equal Opportunities Policy with specialist staff to ensure it is implemented. ProTraining has a record of successful implementation of its published policy, which applies to all its activities. Direct or indirect discrimination in terms of recruitment, employment and education, or any form of harassment, based on gender, ethnic origin, socio-economy background, disability, religious beliefs, trade union membership, family circumstances, sexual orientation, age or any other such distinction is strictly prohibited.[24]

This policy will affect all aspects of project delivery including staff recruitment to the project, beneficiary recruitment, delivery of training and support and monitoring and evaluation activities[25]. The project will actively seek to promote equal opportunities and diversity, and will focus recruitment of beneficiaries on recent entrants or re-entrants to the labour market, people from minority ethnic communities, refugees, women (who are under-represented in the ICT field), people with disabilities and those with care responsibilities. This will have the effect of reducing inequalities in the labour market and will empower individual beneficiaries, giving them greater economic power[26]. It will have the following impacts[27]:

Men and women: recruitment will be designed to maximise the number of female beneficiaries, as women are still under-represented in ICT. *The impact will be more women receiving higher level ICT training, thus increasing the number of women moving into technical ICT jobs.*[28]

Ethnic minorities: a high proportion of beneficiaries on past projects have been from minority ethnic communities. This project aims to have a major impact on these groups, and especially on black-owned businesses who are on average less likely to access mainstream business support and who research shows are more likely to fail. *The impact will be that people from ethnic minority communities will receive higher level ICT training, thus increasing their employability and economic power, and that black-owned businesses will receive business support and advice, making them more competitive.*

People with disabilities: The project premises are fully accessible, and ProTraining has a robust support mechanism for people with disabilities, thus allowing beneficiaries with disabilities to take full advantage of the training on offer. There will be a specific outreach to employed people with a disability through the partner organisation WellFare. *The impact of these measures will be that people with a disability will receive higher level ICT training, making them more employable and empowering them to apply for promotion or higher paid jobs.*

Promoting Equal Opportunities

This project will positively promote and encourage equal opportunities and diversity awareness through the following measures:

By example Staff and trainers from ProTraining are from a range of backgrounds, with a mix of genders and ages. The project's partner organisation is a black-owned business[29].

Through culturally aware training methods All training will take place in a culturally sensitive context, with full awareness of the different needs and beliefs of beneficiaries – for example making available an appropriate prayer room; availability of Kosher and Halal food. Examples used in training and training materials will embed an awareness of diversity.

By assessing individual skills and needs Each beneficiary will be individually assessed at the recruitment/induction stage, and their individual needs and aspirations taken into account in designing and reviewing their learning programme. This will include any needs in terms of additional learning support, adaptation of learning materials and the learning environment, translation and English Language support etc.[30]

Via positive messages to employers Employers will receive information (marketing, evaluations, mentoring, business advice) that fully reflects cultural diversity in a positive light. Employers will be encouraged to support their employees through the learning process, taking into account their individual circumstances.

In addition, all beneficiaries will be made aware of grievance procedures, including procedures for reporting harassment, at the induction of the programme. Strong measures will be adopted, in line with ProTraining's policy, to deal with any incidents of a discriminatory nature[31].

The project will be monitored regularly to ensure that it is meeting its stated equal opportunities aims in terms of outputs, targets and methodologies. The project Steering Group will take overall charge of this monitoring[32]

 notes

24   The writer is quoting from ProTraining's Equal Opportunities policy to show how broad the policy is.

25   Specific activities of the project are mentioned, to which the policy will be

applied. This is a good first step, but more detail will be required in order to score well.

26 The writer is setting out the positive impacts that the project will have on people who may be under-represented in the field of ICT, and may be at risk of social exclusion in general.

27 Impacts of the project on specific groups are listed. The bid writer has chosen to focus on the groups that are most relevant to the project and the area in which the project is run. Other projects may have found it more appropriate to talk about, for example, people from rural communities, refugees or people over 50.

28 The format for each of the groups listed is to describe the relevant activity and how it will be carried out, and then to state what the impact of this activity will be. This can be a good format for questions of this type, as it makes the impact extremely clear to the scorer.

29 The writer is showing that ProTraining itself is an example of good Equal Opportunities practice and that it has a diverse workplace.

30 An important aspect of diversity is recognising individual differences. This paragraph shows that each beneficiary will be treated as an individual, and that the project will be adapted to meet any particular needs that they have.

31 It is always worth showing, however obvious it may seem, that the project team will take steps to combat any discrimination or harassment that may be experienced during the course of a project.

32 This shows that the effectiveness of the equal opportunities measures will be monitored, and states who will take responsibility for the monitoring.

Beneficiaries

The form then turns its attention to beneficiaries. For most bids, it will be important to show that you understand the needs of the target beneficiaries and have at least some experience of working with them. In addition, you will need to back up your own knowledge with research from outside sources that can be used to demonstrate that your project has been designed to meet the genuine needs of your beneficiaries.

The scoring criteria for this question was very specific:

Describe the barriers the target groups face to progression in the labour market. With reference to your list of outputs in part C of the form, outline the actions you will provide and describe how these actions will help the beneficiaries overcome the barriers identified.

This might look daunting, but in fact it is one of the easier questions to answer. A strategy for answering a question like this would be:

1   Describe the barriers faced by the group (this should involve drawing on outside research or reports)

2   Describe how the project will help the beneficiaries

3   Point out how each of the actions of the project will help the beneficiaries overcome the barrier described in 1.

It is this last step that is the most crucial. Many bid writers will talk at length about the barriers faced by the beneficiary groups, and then go on to say what the project will do as a response, but neglect to point out exactly how these project actions will help the beneficiaries to overcome the barriers, thinking that it is obvious. *It may not be obvious to the scorer* who might have no experience of working with that particular beneficiary group.

Identify the specific target beneficiaries for the project

The target beneficiaries for this project are employees of small businesses[33] especially those at risk due to technological and structural change. One of the major barriers to progression faced by small business employees is a lack of organisational investment in training, especially training for wider and future skills needs[34]. This does not only hamper individual employee career prospects but acts as a brake on the business as a whole[35].

A recent UK study into the barriers faced by small businesses in training their workforce stated: 'For employers, the first consideration is often the cost. Secondary issues include paying for training provision and time off work and staff time to administer and support training and learning.' (http://lll.veb.it) These findings have been demonstrated on a local level through the 'Small Business Learning' research project in the North of the region.

In addition, the pan-European study 'Small Business Training and Competitiveness' found that 'small businesses find training courses too broad in scope, failing to meet their specialised needs' (PJB Associates 2001)[36].

This project will address these barriers in the following way:

■ linking the need for advanced IT training to business plan priorities, thus ensuring that customised training can be provided[37]. This will be done through one-to-one inductions involving beneficiaries and their employing organisations. This induction will identify the specific skills needs of the beneficiaries in relation to their job role and the business plan of their employing organisation[38]. It will allow a customised programme of training and support to be designed that meets employer needs as much as employee needs, thus removing the barrier associated with lack of employer support for training[39].

- training provided free of charge to employers and employees, thus removing the barrier of cost

- training provided on a flexible schedule, including the use of open and distance learning, to address the barrier of lack of time

- individual training and development plans for beneficiaries to allow them to track their own learning development and to encourage them to set their own learning goals for the project and beyond

The project will enable individual beneficiaries to progress within the labour market by updating their skills in a key growth area, thus increasing their future employability and economic potential[40]. This will be particularly important to beneficiaries from groups that may face additional disadvantages in the labour market, including members of black and minority ethnic groups and refugee communities[41].

notes

33   The bid writer starts by stating who the beneficiaries are. Don't be afraid to state the obvious! The people scoring or assessing the bid will only have a short time to come to a conclusion and will have seen many other bids that day, so it is always a good idea to keep pointing out the basic facts of the project as you go along.

34   The scorer states the main barrier to progression in the labour market for the target group.

35   The consequences of this barrier are pointed out.

36   The writer uses three different sources to demonstrate that the barrier that has been identified above is genuine. The two quotes that are given here also have the advantage that they give some explanation of the main barrier (that small businesses do not train their staff) by pointing out the reasons behind it.

37   The first part of each bullet point states briefly what the project will do.

38   The second part describes how it will do it.

39 Finally, it describes the impact of the actions and the barrier(s) that the actions will help to overcome.

40 The writer goes on to point out how the project will help not only the small businesses but also their individual employees. This is important, because it is the employees who will be receiving the most direct support from the project activities rather than the businesses. It balances out some of the statements above that talk more about benefits to the small businesses involved.

41 The importance of the project to particular groups is pointed out – these are group that the RDA has stated in its strategic documents that it wants to target for additional support. The bid writer is demonstrating a good knowledge of RDA strategies with this comment.

The next question is about how beneficiaries will be recruited to the project. This type of question often crops up on bidding forms because under-recruitment is a huge problem in some projects, and is one of the major reasons that projects fail. No funding body wants to back a failing project, and so you will need to convince them that you have a well thought out strategy for recruiting enough beneficiaries from the right target group.

The scoring criteria for this question were as follows:

Set out the recruitment method for the target group and show how it is appropriate to their needs. Describe the measures in place to ensure that the project can successfully retain beneficiaries, with reference to the needs and barriers outlined above.

Perhaps the most important, and overlooked, part of this scoring criteria is: 'show how it is appropriate to their needs'. Even experienced organisations can go wrong with questions like this, because they are so used to working with the particular beneficiary group that they assume that their needs are obvious. They may also think that their experience in delivering projects in the past speaks for itself. Past experience can say a lot, but it is always necessary to explain why recruitment is carried out a certain way and why this is successful, rather than just stating past success.

This question is also about **retention** – making sure that people don't drop out of the project. This can be just as important as recruitment. If too many beneficiaries drop out before they have completed their time on the project, then the project is not very likely to meet its outputs.

State how you intend to recruit beneficiaries to your project and retain them once on it

Recruitment

ProTraining has a track record of recruiting and retaining beneficiaries from small businesses to a variety of publicly funded and commercial training and development projects. Over the last 2 years it has trained 200 small business employees and has carried out business audits on 60 businesses[42].

Specific measures used to recruit beneficiaries to this project will include:

- Press advertising targeting both employers and employees to raise awareness of the project

- Working with partner agencies such as Business Link, Chamber of Commerce, the Regional Sector Groups, and the Training Network, with whom ProTraining has a long-standing working relationship

- Presentations to employers e.g. through business breakfast seminars and sector-specific press articles

It will be important to target employers as well as employees, because employers have the final say as to whether their employees can be released for training. Convincing the employers that this project will help their business to grow will be the key to recruiting beneficiaries. However, small business owners and managers do not have time to respond to every offer of training and support that comes through their door[43]. The report *Business Growth – A Study on the Effectiveness of Business Support Agencies* has shown that employer-led organisations such as the Chamber of Commerce and the Regional Sector Groups have the most influence over whether employers will engage with business support projects such as this one (see p23). Working with these organisations has been show to be far more effective than mailshots in recruiting business people to projects (see p 43)[44]. Therefore the project team will spend time with representatives from both of these agencies promoting the project and gaining their support[45].

Retention

ProTraining's experience has shown that the key factors in retention among employed beneficiaries are flexibility, motivation, relevance to work role and career aspirations. This has been discovered through beneficiary feedback and evaluation from past projects, and is further demonstrated by reports such as the PJB

Associates report quoted above. An additional factor in retention is a high level of client service on the part of the project team, and again this has been highlighted by feedback from past beneficiaries[46]. Bearing this in mind the project will have the following measures in place to maximise retention.

- Consultation with employers to ensure that they support employee learning
- Regular reviews of learning plans to promote continued motivation
- Flexibility of training timetable, including arranging training sessions at times to suit beneficiaries and maximising the use of open, distance and online learning

When similar measures were put in place in the 'Small Business Managers' project, the drop-out rate fell by 40% (see external evaluator's report)[47].

notes

42   The writer is giving details of relevant experience. Notice that only the experience of ProTraining in working with small businesses is quoted here, even though the organisation has also provided training for other groups, such as women returners to the labour market.

43   This shows the needs of the target group…

44   …justifies these needs with appropriate research…

45   …and outlines the strategies that will be used to meet the needs.

46   The writer uses a combination of internal and external research to highlight the factors that the project team believes are important in retaining beneficiaries.

47   The effectiveness of these measures is demonstrated by showing the impact they had on a previous project. This shows the importance of a good monitoring strategy for projects, as it allows project improvement to be documented for future reference.

The project plan

Many funding bodies have now started to ask for a summary project plan in order to demonstrate that the project has been well thought out and designed. The funding body asks for the following in its scoring criteria:

a   Marks will be awarded to projects that set out a delivery plan that is realistic and sets out milestones with clear deadlines.

b   Applicants should state delivery methods to be used and show how these are appropriate for the target groups.

c   A management structure for the project should be presented.

d   Applicants should also describe systems that will be in place to manage data, finance and resources, and should identify how the project would deal with any deviation from the delivery plan.

e   Quality standards that the organisation currently works to should be stated.

This is a lot of information to convey in one page! Good preparation and planning is the key here. If you have gone through all the stages of planning the project, it should be relatively easy to summarise any aspect of the project plan to meet the scoring criteria. However, if you have skipped planning, this could be one of the hardest questions to answer and your answer might not be very convincing. The moral is: don't try to cut corners with planning, it will be obvious to the scorers!

Explain how you intend to deliver and manage the project

This project will be managed and delivered in accordance with standards set up by ProTraining for project management. The management structure can be summarised as follows[48]:

- **Steering Group** to provide an overview of project delivery and to ensure good fit with relevant regional and sector-specific strategies. The Steering Group will include representatives from SMEs and from employer representation groups.

- **Project Director** to provide strategic input to the project and overall direction to the operation of the project.

- **Project Manager** to manage and monitor delivery to target and to auditable standards. The project manager will have overall responsibility for resource management, record-keeping, financial probity and data management.

- **Project Delivery Team** includes specialist trainers and ourtreach workers from ProTraining and from its partner organisations. The team includes administrators experienced in the support of ESF, SRB and LIF projects

■ **Project Support Unit** to provide overall monitoring, quality management and general management checks on project delivery. This team will also commission auditors to verify project financial records.

The nominated project manager is working towards a project management qualification[49]. Project delivery will follow standards and methods for record keeping and finance set out in the European Social Fund Good Practice Guide[50]. Project data will be maintained by the administrative team in line with organisational policy and the Data Protection Act[51]. The project manager will initially be responsible for dealing with deviation from the project schedule, and the Steering Group will take action on major deviation or slippage.

Project delivery will follow the methodology developed by the ProTraining team over the last 5 years. This project will be delivered on a 6-month cycle of intake, with the last two cohorts overlapping so as to ensure that the project completes by the end of the funding period and that beneficiaries get maximum support from the project during its life time especially in relation to the online support via email. Within each 6-month cycle, the delivery schedule will be as follows[52]:

Month 1:   Inductions and one-to-one sessions with beneficiaries to ensure that the project meets their individual needs as employees.

Technology site visits to employers, with mentoring and advice offered to ensure that businesses are given the individual support they need to improve their use of ICT

Month 2-4: Flexible training offered; individual training plans

Month 5-6: Beneficiary completes work based project (negotiated with employer to meet business needs) with mentoring support from tutor.

There will also be online support via email throughout the lifetime of the project to ensure that beneficiaries are fully supported throughout their training in a way that fits around the demands of their job.

Setup and Recruitment: April – July 2003[53]

Production of marketing materials; presentation to employers and employer organisations; referrals through business networks such as Business Link

Cohort 1: August – December 2003

Milestone: 30 beneficiaries trained by December 2003

Special meeting of Steering Group to discuss updates and refinements Dec 2003

Cohort 2: January – July 2004

Milestone: 60 beneficiaries in total trained by July 2004

Milestone: Interim evaluation April 2004

Cohort 3: July – November 2004

Milestone: 90 beneficiaries in total trained by November 2004

Evaluation: December 2004

ProTraining works to industry Quality Assurance standards and is subject to ALI inspection. It is accredited by the BCS to run ECDL and Advanced ECDL, and is an accredited Microsoft Academy[54]

notes

48 The writer has started by tackling item c of the scoring criteria. The management structure shows how beneficiaries and employers are involved in the management of the project. Showing an appropriate level of community involvement (including beneficiary representatives) is becoming more important. This section clearly shows the responsibilities of the individuals and groups mentioned.

49 This has not been specifically asked for in the scoring criteria, but helps to demonstrate the commitment of ProTraining to quality and high standards.

50 The writer is showing that standards and methods to be used for the project follow the appropriate guidelines for dealing with this type of funding. This partially addresses part d of the scoring criteria.

51 It is always worthwhile to mention that your project conforms to any relevant legislation, as this shows your awareness of the laws that will affect your project activity and reassures the funding body of the high quality standards of your organisation.

52 The next section highlights some of the methods that will be used to achieve the project aims, and states briefly how these meet the needs of beneficiaries. This addresses part b of the scoring criteria. However, space restrictions meant that in practice the bid writer could not go into the level of detail that she wanted about this aspect of the project.

53 Part a of the scoring criteria has been addressed here by briefly listing the different stages of the project and the milestones (with dates) that will be achieved within each stage. This will not be the most appropriate way for every project. For example projects with a rolling intake of beneficiaries will not naturally fall into stages like this. However, all projects should have milestones that will be achieved at intervals throughout their lifetime. Listing these in order will give the scorer an idea of the project schedule and demonstrates that the project has been well planned. In some cases you may want to attach a PERT

chart or similar to your bid to show that the project has been planned in detail.

54   The answer to part e of the scoring criteria includes all quality accreditations relevant to this project. If your organisation does not work to any quality standards, this may be something that is worth investigating. For example, Investors in People is a good demonstration that an organisation is dedicated to training and developing its staff, and is extremely relevant to any organisation that offers training to others. All organisations that offer any kind of training now come under the Adult Learning Inspectorate (ALI) and will need to arrange for regular inspections. This is a useful quality standard to quote in a bid, especially if you have scored well in a previous inspection.

Exit strategy

In the final example from the Web Support Project bid, the team has been asked to explain how the project will continue once the funding period has ended in two years' time. This is a common question, because funders like to know that the funding given to projects will have a lasting impact that will go beyond the time period for which the funding is actually given. This is sometimes known as the **exit strategy** for the project.

How this question is answered depends very much on the nature of the project and its beneficiaries. For projects that work with businesses, it is often appropriate to say that the services given to the businesses will only be supported for a certain amount of time through funding, and that businesses will have to start paying for the services after the project finishes. For other beneficiaries who might not have the means to pay, it would be more appropriate to say that other sources of funding will be found once the current funding runs out. You could list some of the funds that might be approached.

The ProTraining team has gone for the first option in answering this question:

> **Explain the measures you have in place for the continuation of the project**
>
> The exit strategy for the project has been mapped out in advance. After the end of the funding period, this project will be offered to SMEs on a 'pay as you go' basis as an alternative to engaging consultants or media design companies to carry out web design

> and marketing work on a subcontracted basis. The team believes that once the programme has been fully developed with beneficiary feedback and employer input, it will make an attractive alternative both in terms of cost and in terms of building internal capacity within SMEs. It will continue to contribute towards regional regeneration and economic development aims, but will no longer require public funding to support its delivery and continued development.

As you can see, the bid writer has tried to convey to the scoring panel that the funding will have an ongoing impact in the region.

There is no mention in this particular question of what will happen to the current beneficiaries once the funding has ended – whether they will be given any kind of aftercare or ongoing support. Some bidding forms do ask this question and expect project teams to have thought about the ongoing welfare of their beneficiaries. Strategies may include using other sources of funding within the organisation to offer ongoing advice and mentoring to beneficiaries, or referring beneficiaries to other projects or partners in the local area that might be able to help them further.

Other kinds of bidding form

The following are extracts from bidding forms relating to very different kinds of funding. These are designed to give you an idea of the different styles of question you may encounter. As with the examples above, notes have been added to highlight some of the important points.

How will the grant requested be used?

(Please provide a breakdown of how the grant will be used. For example, if you are using the grant for staffing costs and running costs let us know what those costs are, break them down into things like rent, heating, lighting, what staff are being employed and for how much etc).

How will you check that you have successfully carried out the activities described above?

(Please include here details of how you will measure success e.g. through project monitoring, user surveys, management appraisals etc.).

These questions were taken from a Local Authority grant aid scheme for the voluntary sector. As you can see, they relate very closely to the information in a project plan and so organisations that have invested time in planning are likely to be able to answer these questions well.

Please outline the three main qualitative aims of your project.

These should define the changes/achievements you hope to make during the course of the project.

This question above was taken from a New Opportunities Fund bidding form. A question such as this gives bidders an opportunity to talk about the 'soft outcomes' and overall achievements of the project, rather than the usual 'number of people trained, number of jobs created' type of output.

Please complete the following two sentences using no more than 25 words for each.

The work to be funded aims to...

We want to use our grant to pay for...

The above questions were set by a charitable trust to help applicants structure their applications for funding. As you can see, they are very similar to the types of question set in chapter 2 to help you develop your project plan. Charitable trusts as a general rule tend to set simpler (and clearer!) questions than the larger funding schemes.

Explain why the project is needed.

Your answer should fully take into account the three points listed below. You will be scored against these points.

- ■ You should provide local detailed evidence and, if appropriate, evidence from a particular sector to support your proposed activity. This can include labour market evidence, local surveys and consultation with employees – including Skills Foresight reports if appropriate.

- ■ You should describe the barriers faced by the target groups and how your project will help to overcome these barriers.

- ■ You should show how your project links with or complements government strategies or initiatives.

In contrast, the question above is highly complex and requires a lot of research. This is taken from an older European Social Fund bidding form and perhaps demonstrates why ESF was mostly taken up by larger organisations, and encouraged the growth of bidding consultancies.

Summary tips

There is a wide range of different questions that can be asked on forms, but they tend to follow similar patterns and fall into distinct categories. There are key strategies that can be used to answer these questions, and many of these have been outlined above.

The following tips summarise some of the good practice points for bidders.

Read the bid documents

It is surprising how few people actually read the guidance documents provided by the funding body thoroughly. These are the key to understanding what those who will be scoring the bids are looking for. However, guidance documents can be long and full of technical terms. If you are a first-time bidder it is highly recommended that you ask the advice of a more experienced colleague, or attend a bidding workshop. The more you understand the background and purpose behind the bidding round, the better you will be able to target the bid.

Answer the questions that are asked

As for an exam, it is of vital importance to answer the question that is actually being asked rather than the question you think is being asked. If you are in any doubt about the purpose of a particular question, seek advice.

Think like a scorer

Putting yourself in the place of the person who will be scoring or assessing the bid will give you an insight into how to write your answers. At all times, write briefly and clearly and avoid the use of jargon. Break longer answers into sections. If you are able, get a copy of the scoring guidelines or criteria and ensure that your answer addresses all of the points that a scorer will be looking for.

Be realistic

The bidding stage is the time to be as critical as possible about the project that has been proposed. In particular, avoid producing a bid that hits all the scoring points but exaggerates what can be achieved – or you will be left with a project that can't be delivered. Especially, be realistic about costings, beneficiary numbers and the time it will take to deliver the project.

Review the bid

Before the bid is submitted, ask someone who has not been involved with the bid preparation process to read it through. If possible, give them a copy of the scoring criteria and ask them to carry out a mock scoring exercise. This will give you valuable feedback as to how the bid reads to someone external.

CHAPTER FOUR

What happens next?

After the writing

It's tempting to think that once you've done the hard work of writing the bid in time for the deadline then that's it. Actually, it's just the start! This short chapter will look at some of the things you need to consider once the bid has been written.

Submitting the bid

The bid has been written and proof read and you're feeling confident about it... This the point at which it's vitally important to ensure that you submit the bid correctly, or all the work might go to waste.

For the larger bidding rounds, it is common for the funding body to request certain documents from your organisation so that they can carry out a risk assessment as part of the scoring process. These may include:

- Your organisation's accounts
- Copies of insurance certificates
- Copies of equal opportunities and health and safety policies
- Letters of support from partners

If you do not submit the documents required, your bid may not even be considered for scoring, so it's important to plan in advance. Letters of support can sometimes cause difficulties because bid writers do not spend enough time at the planning stage getting the real support of the organisations who are put down on the form as the project partners, and so there is a scramble just before the deadline to get the letters of support together. Obviously the sooner you can get these, the better.

In fact the earlier you start planning all round the better. If any of the documents is missing, it may some take time to find or write it. For example, organisations have failed to get funding because their insurance had lapsed, or their equal opportunities policy was not up to date. If you can ensure that all the documents you need are in place well in advance of the deadline, you can then concentrate on writing the bid.

Another important point, as obvious as it sounds, is to make sure you know when the deadline is, get your bid in on time. Funding bodies that set a deadline can be extremely strict about enforcing it, especially when there are a lot of bids to deal with. Even a few minutes past the deadline can result in the bid being rejected. Not all funders are as strict as this, but it is always best to err on the side of caution.

Appeals

Hopefully things will go to plan and your project will be funded. But if things go wrong and your project is not funded, you should be able to ask the funding body for a reason for their decision. Having looked at their reasons, you may feel that you have grounds for an appeal. Funding bodies vary a lot in their approach to appeals, and most issue some kind of guideline about how to go about making an appeal.

There are usually very specific grounds on which you can appeal. Funding bodies that work on a scoring system tend to accept different kinds of appeal than those who use a panel to decide which projects will be funded. In fact projects that are scored can be easier to appeal about, because the feedback tends to be more specific.

If you are appealing against the decision, then you usually have to demonstrate one of the following:

- That the decision was unreasonable, in other words that no reasonable person would have reached that decision

- That there was some bias in the decision, for example a member of the scoring panel had an outside interest that biased him or her in the decision making process

- That the information presented was misunderstood or not properly taken into account

Some funding organisations do not accept appeals at all and it is worth checking in advance or you could end up wasting a lot of time. However, if you have grounds to believe that there was a serious case of professional misconduct during the course of the scoring or assessment process you will always have the right to complain.

Contract negotiation

Once a project has been approved for funding, there may be a period of contract negotiation in which the full conditions of the funding and the project are agreed between the funding body and your organisation.

If your project is approved, it is possible that you will be awarded a smaller amount of money than you asked for. At this point it is important to review your project plan and work out what you can actually do for the money you've been given – or even if the project is still viable. In particular you will need to review your project budget and the outputs you can deliver for the money.

The funding body may at this stage carry out additional checks on your organisation to ensure that you have the resources to carry out the project and that all your systems and policies are in order.

You should be aware that there could be a delay before a final decision is given that the funding has been awarded, and this could have implications for the cash flow situation in your organisation.

Funding strategy

Winning funding for your project is a great achievement and can make all the difference to your organisation. If your organisation has run a lot of funded projects then your project may form part of their strategy for raising external funding to support its work. However, if this is the first funded project your organisation (or department) has run, you may want to think about developing a funding strategy for the future.

A funding strategy sits alongside an organisation's business plan or development plan. It will normally set out what activities within the organisation will be seeking grant funding (this could be all of them!) and what types of funding will be targeted. This will allow you to match projects to suitable types of funding and plan in advance for future bidding rounds. It also helps to ensure that projects needing match funding can be covered by a suitable mix of different funding types.

Finding help

There are a number of organisations that are prepared to give free help to people putting together project bids. For voluntary and community sector organisations, local Voluntary Service Councils are often able to offer support. They are sometimes willing to give support to organisations from other sectors too, but this is by no means guaranteed. Private sector businesses may be able to get support from Business Link.

The funding bodies themselves are often prepared to offer help for potential bidders. Charitable trusts will usually have a helpline or will invite bidders to discuss their ideas with a member of the team before submitting a bid. For larger bidding rounds, there are usually bidding workshops or training days available. You should attend these if at all possible, even if you are an experienced bid writer, as they will point out the unique features of the bidding round and answer any questions. It is also a good way to gain an idea of the other organisations that will be bidding and what their projects are.

Finally, there are a number of businesses and individuals who offer bidding consultancy. These can be invaluable if you have a strong idea for a project but feel that you don't have the time or experience to write it yourself. Charges can be high, but some consultants will work on a 'no win no fee' basis. There are certain things to consider if you are thinking about hiring a consultant. Choosing between different consultants can be tricky. If in doubt, ask for a written quotation and terms of service from each of the consultants you are considering before you make your decision. The following checklist may help you.

- What is the success rate of the consultancy? If it is a larger consultancy, what is the track record of the individual consultant you will be working with?

- Do they have experience of working with the particular fund you are applying for? Some funds are very new or unusual, in which case you will be looking for a broad experience.

- Are they prepared to work closely with you and learn about the details of your project? If not, you may end up with a formula bid that does not describe your project very well, and that is hard for you to actually deliver once the funding has been secured.

- Are they clear about their charging structure? Remember that under the regulations for most funds, consultant fees for writing bids are not eligible and therefore cannot be claimed back.

- Will they keep you well informed as the bid is developed? It is important to have good communication with a consultant you are working with, otherwise you can feel that the whole process is outside of your control. A friendly and approachable consultant who wants to keep you involved can be much easier to work with than one who is uncommunicative and prefers to work independently.

Even when working with a consultant, you should be prepared to put in a lot of work yourself. There will be information about the project and your organisation that you will have to provide and so you should make sure you are available to answer questions and provide information while the bid is being written.

A good consultant can significantly improve your chances of winning funding, but it is still the case that the better the project, the better the bid. A good consultant will help you to develop your project idea and carry out some of the planning activities with you. However, it is likely to be much cheaper if you have already planned the project in some detail before talking to the consultant – as long as you are sure that the project fits the restrictions of the funding body and the funding round.

Conclusion

Applying for funding can be time-consuming and difficult. There is a technique to good bid writing, but it is a technique that can be learned and that improves with practice. Proper project planning can make all the difference, and makes for a much better project in the end.

On the positive side, there are sources of help out there, and if you have worked through this book while developing your ideas and your bid, there's every reason to be confident that you will find the funding for your project.

I wish you the best of luck!